SERMON ON THE MOUNT

Sermon on the Mount

a poetic paraphrase

Sarah Hinlicky Wilson

THORNBUSH PRESS

Copyright © 2020 by Sarah Hinlicky Wilson

Based on the Gospel according to St. Matthew 5:1–7:29.

All rights reserved. No part of this publication may be reproduced, distributed or transmitted in any form or by any means, without prior written permission.

Thornbush Press | www.thornbushpress.com

Book Layout © 2017 BookDesignTemplates.com

Cover Design by Geoffrey Bunting Graphic Design

Sermon on the Mount: A Poetic Paraphrase / Sarah Hinlicky Wilson. -- 1st paperback ed.

ISBN 978-1-7352300-0-9

Mountain

5:1–2

    Seeing the crowds
    Jesus ascended the mountain.

    When he sat down,
    his disciples approached him.

    And opening his mouth
    he taught them,

                saying:

Blessed

5:3–12

Blessed: the forlorn and forsaken
the hurting and heartsick
the humane and restrained
the famished and parched
    for righteousness.

Theirs: the kingdom of heaven
the solace and succor
the birthright and reign
the banquet and feast.

Blessed: the clement and kindly
the wholesome and spotless
the steady and peaceful
the tarnished and smeared
    for righteousness.

Theirs: the kindness and clemency
the perceiving and seeing
the adoption and kinship
the kingdom of heaven.

Blessed: you.

Blessed: when they besmirch you
Blessed: when they browbeat you
Blessed: when they accuse you
           due to
           your alliance

with: me.

In that day,
hurray!
Rewards
for the reviled
abide in heaven.

For so they pursued
the prophets before you.

Salt
5:13

You are the salt of the earth.

But if the salt turns stupid,
how will it get resalted?

The salutary thing
is to fling
it out.

Light
5:14–16

You are the light of the world.

Secret cities don't sit
   on mountaintops.
Lighted lamps don't lurk
   under measuring cups.

So
light your lamp.
Hang it high.

Those you illumine
   will give glory to God in heaven.

The Law and the Prophets
5:17–20

    Don't imagine that
    I came
    to unravel
    the law and the prophets.
    I came
    not to unravel
    but to knit back together.

    I promise you:

    Until heaven and earth perish
    neither the dot of an i
    nor the stroke of a serif
    will perish from the law

    until all the things that are going to happen
    happen.

So
whoever frays the edge of
the least little commandment
and urges folks to do the same
will be sheared off the kingdom of heaven.

But
whoever stitches them up
and urges folks to do the same
will be woven into the kingdom of heaven.

Unless you are of uncut cloth
seamless
smooth
and whole
you will not grace
the banquet tables of heaven.

Killing

5:21–26

You've heard how
the first folks were told:
Don't kill.
 Whoever kills is gonna get it.

But I promise you:

Anyone who snarls
at her nearest and dearest
is gonna get it.

Anyone who growls
at his next of kin,
"You bastard,"
is gonna get it in court.

Anyone who sneers,
"You moron,"
is gonna get it in hell.

So
if you're writing a check for charity
or chanting along in church
and remember how a relative
has cause to be cross at you—

Stop everything.
Get out of there.
Work things out.

Then your worship will be worthwhile.

Make nice with the opposition
and do it quick
en route

or else

they'll give you to the judge,
and the judge to the guard,
and the guard to the jail.

I promise you:
You won't escape
till you pay back

every
last
penny.

Adulterating
5:27–30

You've heard how they were told:
Don't mess around with another man's wife.

But what I say is,
everyone who looks at a woman
(you know how I mean)
already adulterates her in his heart.

So if your right eye wrongs her,
gouge it out and get rid of it.
Better one part perishes
than the whole in hell.

And if your right hand wrongs her,
hack it off and hurl it away.
Better one part perishes
than the whole in hell.

Divorcing

5:31–32

And they were told:
Whoever divorces his wife,
do it nice and legal.

But what I say is,
everyone who divorces his wife
(except on account of her messing around
with another woman's husband)
adulterates her

and whoever marries a divorced woman
adulterates himself.

Swearing
5:33–37

Again, you're aware
they were told: Beware!
Grant God what you swear
in your prayer.

But I declare:
Do not swear!

Not by heaven. It is God's chair.
Not by earth. His feet rest there.
Do not swear by anywhere.
No, not even by your hair.

More than "yes" or "no" is to err
beyond repair.

Nondefiance
5:38–41

> Eye for eye.
> Tooth for tooth.
> Fair is fair.
>
> But what I say is,
> don't defy your foe.
>
> Whoever gives you a right hook,
> offer him an uppercut.
>
> Whoever sues for your overcoat,
> hand him also your undershirt.
>
> Whoever makes you walk one mile,
> lead him on for two.

Giving and Lending
5:42

They ask?
You give.

They borrow?
You lend.

Enemies

5:43–47

The rules plainly state:
Friends are to love;
Enemies, to hate.

Your Father above
says, as I say, to you:
Enemies are to love

And those who harm you.
Your Father above
Sends down the rain

On all, out of love,
Just and unjust the same,
And his sun up above.

His sons act likewise.
For what if you love
Only those, in your eyes,

Who are good? Far above
Basic pay will you get?
It's your brothers you love.

Does this goodwill set
You a notch up above?
Love only for these

Is a small kind of love.
Love your enemies,
Like your Father above.

Perfection
5:48

So
be
perfect,

like
your
Father
in
heaven
is
perfect.

Righteousness

6:1

See to it that
your righteousness
is not seen.

Recognized righteousness
goes unrewarded.

Almsgiving
6:2–4

So
when you give alms
don't give an almighty *BLAST*
like the hypocrites do
in the alleys and avenues
to be praised by people.

I guarantee you,
they've gotten everything they're gonna get.

But as for you,
when you're giving alms,
it's sinister to see
what your own self is doing.

Keep it covered.
And your Father,
hidden in heaven,
will balance the books.

Praying
6:5–8

And
when you pray
don't be like the hypocrites
who have to assemble
in the alleys and avenues
so others observe them.

I guarantee you,
they've gotten everything they're gonna get.

But as for you,
when you pray,
go into your closet and close it.

Keep it covered.
And your Father,
hidden in heaven,
will pay attention
to your petition.

And when you pray
don't *b-b-b-blather* like the *b-b-b-barbarians*
who believe their logorrhea
makes their listeners listen.

Don't be like them.

Your Father
knows what you need
before you even ask.

Our Father
6:9–13

Here's how you should pray.

Our Father
in heaven

holy—be your name
here—come your kingdom
heaven—do on earth

tomorrow's bread
bestow today

when we release
our debtors,
release us
from our debts

spare us the trial
spare us the test
save us from evil
and all of the rest!

Forgiving
6:14–15

Forgive others,
and your Father will forgive you.

Refrain from forgiving others,
and your Father will refrain from forgiving you.

Fasting
6:16–18

And when you fast
don't do like
the frowny faces do
so folks know they're fasting.

I guarantee you,
they've gotten everything they're gonna get.

But when you fast
wash up,
stand up,
chin up,
so no one knows.

Keep it covered.
And your Father,
hidden in heaven,
will repay your pangs.

Treasure

6:19–21

Many treasure treasure
   on earth where
moths munch on it
decay devours it
robbers ransack it.

If you treasure treasure
   in heaven where
moths are missing
decay is denied
robbers are refused,

you will cherish
what won't perish.

Darkness
6:22–23

The lamp of your life is your eye.

So
if your eye is laser-focused
your whole being is bright.

But
if your eye is evil
your whole being is dark.

So
if the light in you
is darkness—

> **how great
> the darkness**

Lords

6:24

You can't obey two lords
at the same time.

You'll hate the one
and love the other
or
you'll support the one
and undermine the other.

You can't obey both
God and Gold.

Sparrows
6:25–26

Which is why I say:

Don't pull yourself apart with
"what'll I eat?" or "what'll I wear?"
Isn't your soul greater than its sustenance
and your figure than its finery?

Sparrows don't sow.
Robins don't reap.
Blackbirds don't build barns.

Yet your Father in heaven
harbors the birds of heaven
under his wings.

You goose!
Aren't you worth more than a warbler?

Lilies

6:27–30

Does pulling yourself apart
add height to your heels?
And concerning clothing,
why pull yourself apart?

Learn from the lilies,
which without spinning or sewing grow.

What I'm saying is,
even Solomon in all his fancy finery
couldn't compare to a simple speedwell
or a plain old pink.

So if God decks out
the dandelions and daffodils
that are blooming today
and mown down tomorrow,
won't he do more for you?

Such feeble faith!

First
6:31–33

So
don't pull yourself apart with
"What'll we eat?" or
"What'll we drink?" or
"What'll we wear?"

The heathen are always on the hunt for these things,
as if your Father in heaven
didn't already know
you need them.

First
scope out your Father's kingdom
and survey his righteousness.

Then
all these things
will be annexed to your acreage.

Tomorrow

6:34

So
don't pull yourself apart
over tomorrow.
Tomorrow can pull itself apart
just fine on its own.

Today's troubles
are more than enough.

Damning

7:1–2

Don't damn
so you won't be damned.

For what you dam up
will be denied you, too,

and the meter you mete out
will be meted out to you.

Twig and Beam
7:3–5

Do you see a twig in your brother's eye? Yes
Have you checked your own eye? No
Check it

Is there a beam in your eye? No
Check again

Is there a beam in your eye? Yes
Remove it

Is the beam still in your eye? Yes
Try again

Is the beam still in your eye? No
Is the twig still in your brother's eye? Yes
Remove it

Pearls and Pigs
7:6

Don't give the holy
to the hounds,

nor toss your pearls
to the pigs,

lest they trample them,
and turn,
and tackle you!

Ask Seek Knock
7:7–11

Ask and you'll receive.
Seek and you'll find.
Knock and you'll be welcomed in.

Everyone who asks receives.
Everyone who seeks finds.
Everyone who knocks is welcomed in.

However evil, will any of you,
if your child asks for bread,
hand over a stone?

However wicked, will any of you,
if your child asks for fish,
hand over a snake?

If you can be good to yours,
how much more will your
Father in heaven
be good to you
if you
        ask
                seek
                        knock!

The Law and the Prophets
7:12

    So
    all the things
    you wish people
    would do for you,

    you
    do first
    for them.

    This
    is the law and the prophets.

Gate
7:13–14

    Head for the strait gate,
    for broad is the boulevard
    and wide is the way
    that leads to death.
        Hordes hasten
        to destruction.

    But strait is the gate
    and wearisome the way
    that leads to life.
        Some seek.
        Few find.

Wolves
7:15

Look out for pseudoprophets:

working through the countryside,
sneaking up alongside,
sheep on the outside,
wolves on the inside,
greedy at your graveside.

Grapes and Figs
7:16–20

From their fruits you will recognize them.

For are grapes *(Vitis vinifera)*
gathered from an acanthus *(Acanthus syriacus)*
or figs *(Ficus carica)*
from a puncture vine *(Tribulus terrestris)*?

Good tree ⇒ fair fruit.
Rotten tree ⇒ evil fruit.

Good tree ⇏ evil fruit.
Rotten tree ⇏ fair fruit.

∴ Rotten tree ⇒ fire.

Yes, from their fruits you will recognize them.

Lord! Lord!
7:21–23

    Not all who say
    Lord! Lord!
    enter the kingdom.
    But you workers-of-the-will of my Father:
    come in.

    Many will say
    Lord! Lord!
    open the kingdom!

    Did we not speak out—
        all in your name?
    Did we not cast out—
        all in your name?
    Did we not act out—
        all in your name?

    Then I will say
    Never! Ever!
    enter the kingdom.
    You laborers-of-lawlessness:
    depart.

Rock
7:24–25

So
everyone who hears these words of mine
and does them
will be like a sage
who built a house on a rock.

And the rain fell
and the rivers came
and the winds blew.

And they struck that house.

And the house did not fall,
for it was built on a rock.

Sand
7:26–27

And
everyone who hears these words of mine
and does not do them
will be like a fool
who built a house on the sand.

And the rain fell
and the rivers came
and the winds blew.

And they struck that house.

And it fell.

And great
        was the fall
                of that house.

Dumbfounded

7:28–29

And when it happened that
Jesus finished all these words,

the crowds were
dumbfounded
by his teaching;

for he was teaching
like the one who had
authored all these things,
and not like one of their experts.

Sarah Hinlicky Wilson
is the Founder of Thornbush Press.
She serves as Associate Pastor at
Tokyo Lutheran Church in Japan,
where she lives with her husband and son.
She co-hosts the podcast
"Queen of the Sciences:
Conversations between a Theologian
and Her Dad" with Paul R. Hinlicky.
Sign up for her quarterly e-newsletter
"Theology & a Recipe"
and learn more about her other books at:

www.sarahhinlickywilson.com

and

www.thornbushpress.com

by the same author

Pearly Gates:
Parables from the Final Threshold

A Guide to Pentecostal Movements for Lutherans

Woman, Women, and the Priesthood
in the Trinitarian Theology of Elisabeth Behr-Sigel

www.ingramcontent.com/pod-product-compliance
Lightning Source LLC
Chambersburg PA
CBHW021133080526
44587CB00012B/1276